STAMPEDE!

Poems to Celebrate the WILD SIDE of School

by
Laura Purdie Salas

Illustrated by
Steven Salerno

CLARION BOOKS
NEW YORK

Swarm

We crowd the empty schoolyard,
a flood of bumblebees.
We buzz and flitter-tumble,
trade gossip on the breeze.

I brought a kickball—
want to play?
I wonder what's
for lunch today.

When the doors swing open wide,
we bumblebees all fly inside.

New Mouse

Go left, then right.
Wrong turns, dead ends.
Can't find my class.
I've got no friends.

Each hallway is
a hallway clone.
Can't find my way
around alone.

A thousand halls,
a thousand ways,
I'm lost inside
this new-school maze.

Whole Hog

I'm jumping in puddles left after the rain.
The best ones are deep, dark, and BIG!

I'm clomping and stomping and splashing to school,
just messing around like a pig.

There's goop sliding down from my nose to my toes.
I'm tracking the mucky stuff in.

The gym teacher asks if I rolled in the mud.
"I wish!" I reply with a grin.

Rumble, Grumble, Growl

Hear my stomach rumble.
Hear my stomach roar.
The noise drowns out the teacher.
My belly's getting sore.

I'm a starving bear in springtime—
a bear who's slept too long.
My brain feels slow and foggy.
My appetite is strong.

I'd love some peanut butter
to jolt my brain awake.
But I'm not a picky eater—
I'll take chips or fruit or cake!

8

Tomorrow Is Picture Day?

I'm missing three teeth, there's a scratch by my eye.
I trimmed my own bangs—and I cut *way* too high.

My dad says a butterfly's blooming in me,
but a hideous caterpillar's all that I see.

Nesting

I'm one quiet fox.
My desk is my den,
with quizzes, smooth rocks, and
a note from a friend.

I tuck deep inside
the hollowed-out wood
to make me feel safe when I'm
not understood.

Blush

The whisper
spreads like
fire or
flu.

"Someone has
a crush
on you!"

My cheeks burn
hot as a
sun-sharp
ray.

I'm a blazing
cardinal,
winging
away.

Ducks in a Row

Do you all
      Understand how we walk while in school?
     Children, listen!
       Keep quiet's the number one rule.
      Leave the lockers alone and
       I'm sure you'll do fine.
      No poking or
       Giggling—and
        Stay in your line!

Prickly

When I'm feeling
porcupine-y,
I get nasty,
I get whiny.

Stay away or
I might stick you.
My sharp words are
quills to prick you.

Here, Boy!

Lunch bell starts ringing,
down the hallway I bound.
I'm a dog who's just heard
the can-opener sound.

One slice of pizza,
some more meatloaf, please.
Some salad and—*yum*—
ravioli with cheese.

Hamburger patty,
a stick of fried fish.
Keep piling it on—
there's still room on my dish.

Run to the table.
Quick! Hurry! Can't wait
to gulp down my food
and then lick clean my plate.

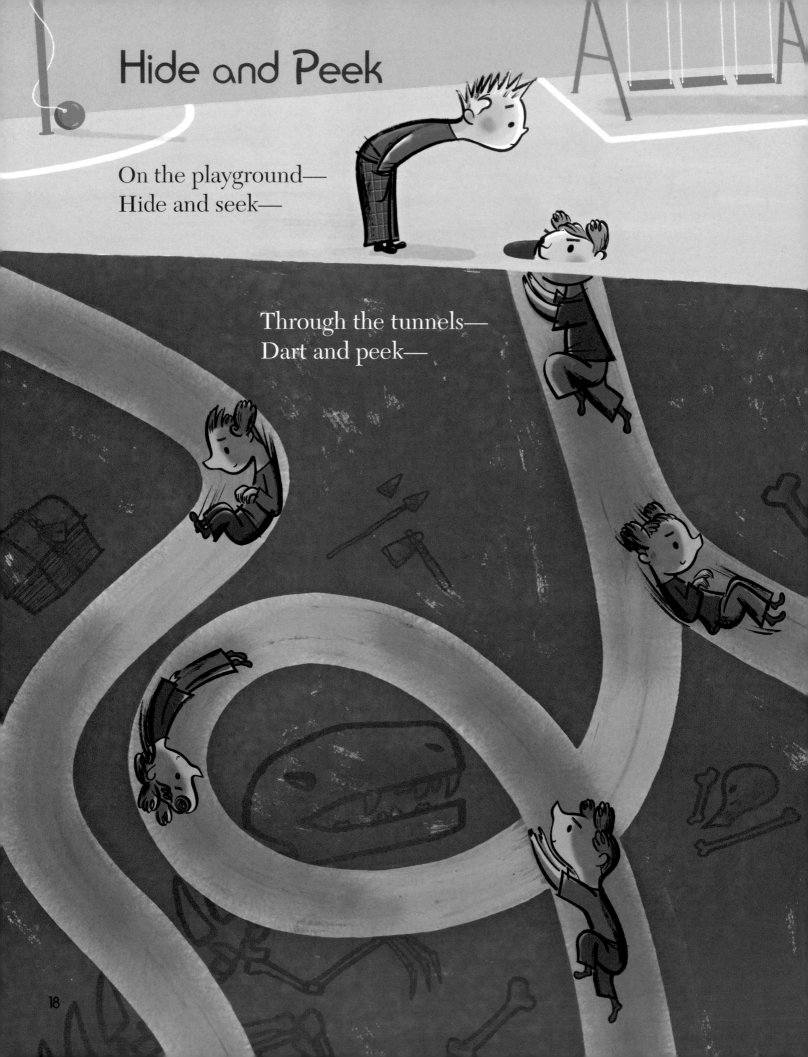

Hide and Peek

On the playground—
Hide and seek—

Through the tunnels—
Dart and peek—

Prairie dogs, we
Pop up here—
Quick—
Glance around—

Then disappear!

20

King of the Jungle (Gym)

From metal branch
to metal vine,
I dip and dive—
this jungle's mine.

Back and forth
I soar and swing.
On monkey bars
I'm Monkey King!

21

Playground Sparrows

In one wave, we fly the coop.
We flood the field, we slide and loop.
We flock together, shout and whoop.
Then school bell rings, and—

no

more

group!

Printer Problems

My pencil scrapes across the paper.
I'm such a lousy letter-shaper.

My hand's as clumsy as a claw.
My letters land like scattered straw.

Erasing leaves a dusty patch.
My writing looks like chicken scratch.

Counting on Me

I've counted up all of my fingers.
This math problem still has me beat.
A centipede's got what I'm missing—
a collection of one hundred feet.

P.U.

At Sharing Time, I looked around
as if I didn't know
who stunk.

But everybody sniffed my way,
and now they yell, "Look out!
It's Skunk!"

Turtleneck

I tuck my face into my sweater,
still as I can be.

I should have studied, but I didn't.
PLEASE—don't call on me.

Stampede!

The last bell rings.
We spill outside,
like captives finally freed.

We're thundering, fumbling
elephants—
an after-school stampede.

30

For Randy, my laughing hyena, who always keeps the faith — L.P.S.

For Amy Jo, Chad, Matthew, Jessica, Jamie, Joe, Steven, Katie, and Jenna,
all delightful animals when they were little ones! — S.S.

Clarion Books
an imprint of Houghton Mifflin Harcourt Publishing Company
215 Park Avenue South, New York, NY 10003
Text copyright © 2009 by Laura Purdie Salas
Illustrations copyright © 2009 by Steven Salerno

The illustrations for this book were created using brushes and gouache on
Arches 260-lb. hot press watercolor paper, and digital enhancements.
The text was set in 18-point New Caledonia.

www.clarionbooks.com

Manufactured in China

Library of Congress Cataloging-in-Publication Data

Salas, Laura Purdie.
Stampede! : poems to celebrate the wild side of school / by Laura Purdie Salas ; illustrated by Steven Salerno.
  p. cm.
ISBN 978-0-618-91488-3
1. School children—Juvenile poetry. 2. Children's poetry, American. I. Salerno, Steven, ill. II. Title.
PS3619.A4256S73 2009
811'.6—dc22
2007050184

WKT 10 9 8 7 6 5 4 3 2 1